Aandologix

By-Krishna Mohan Avancha

How APPLE was started:

The establishment of Apple

The historical backdrop of the universally adored start-up is a tech fantasy of one carport, three companions and exceptionally humble beginnings. Be that as it may, we're losing track of the main issue at hand...

The two Steves - Jobs and Wozniak - may have been Apple's most noticeable originators, yet were it not for their companion Ronald Wayne there may be no iPhone, iPad or iMac today. Occupations persuaded him to take 10% of the organization stock and go about as a judge should he and Woz reach boiling point, yet Wayne pulled out 12 days after the fact, selling for just $500 a holding that would have been worth $72bn 40 years after the fact.

Ron Wayne

How Jobs met Woz

Occupations and Woz (that is Steve Wozniak) were presented in 1971 by a common companion, Bill Fernandez, who proceeded to end up one of Apple's most punctual workers. The two Steves got along gratitude to their common love of innovation and tricks.

Occupations and Wozniak united, at first concocting tricks, for example, fixing up a sketch of a hand appearing center finger to be shown amid a graduaction service at Jobs' school, and a call to the Vatican that almost got them access to the Pope.

The two companions were additionally utilizing their innovation know-how to fabricate 'blue boxes' that made it conceivable to make long separation telephone calls for nothing.

Inclining Articles

Get another iPhone X for under £700 from VERY – here's the secret

Apple may have ended the iPhone X, however it's as yet an extraordinary telephone....

Fueled By

Employments and Wozniak cooperated on the Atari arcade diversion Breakout while Jobs was working at Atari and Wozniak was working at HP - Jobs had restricted Woz into helping him lessen the quantity of rationale chips required. Employments figured out how to get a decent reward for the work on Breakout, of which he gave a little add up to Woz.

The principal Apple PC

The two Steves went to the Homebrew Computer Club together; a PC specialist bunch that accumulated in California's Menlo Park from 1975. Woz had seen his first MITS Altair there - which today looks like minimal in excess of a container of lights and circuit sheets - and was enlivened by MITS' manufacture it-yourself approach (the

Altair came as a unit) to make something less difficult for whatever is left of us. This logic keeps on radiating through in Apple's items today.

So Woz created the main PC with a   like console and the capacity to associate with a normal TV as a screen. Later initiated the Apple I, it was the model of each advanced PC, yet Wozniak wasn't endeavoring to change the world with what he'd created - he simply needed to flaunt the amount he'd figured out how to do with so couple of assets.

Addressing NPR (National Public Radio) in 2006, Woz clarified that "When I constructed this Apple I... the main PC to state a PC should resemble a   - it ought to have a console - and the yield gadget is a TV set, it wasn't generally to demonstrate the world [that] here is the heading [it] ought to go [in]. It was to truly demonstrate the general population around me, to brag, to be cunning, to get affirmation for having structured an exceptionally cheap PC."

Employments and Woz

It nearly didn't occur, however. The Woz we realize now has an overwhelming identity - he's financed shake shows and shimmied on Dancing with the Stars - be that as it may, as he told the Sydney Morning Herald, "I was bashful and felt that I thought minimal about the most current advancements in PCs." He verged on dodging out through and through, and giving the Club a miss.

How about we be grateful he didn't. Employments saw Woz's PC, perceived its brightness, and sold his VW microbus to help support its generation. Wozniak sold his HP adding machine (which cost more than number crunchers do today!), and together they established Apple Computer Inc on 1 April 1976, close by Ronald Wayne.

Why Apple was named Apple

The name Apple was to cause Apple issues in later years as it was awkwardly like that of the Beatles' distributer, Apple Corps, yet its beginning was sufficiently honest.

Addressing Byte magazine in December 1984, Woz acknowledged Jobs for the thought. "He was working every now and then in the plantations up in Oregon. I suspected that it may be on the grounds that there were apples in the plantation or possibly simply its fructarian nature. Perhaps the word coincidentally occurred to him.

Regardless, we both attempted to concoct better names however neither one of us could consider anything better after Apple was referenced."

As indicated by the life story of Steve Jobs, the name was brought about by Jobs after he came back from Macintosh ranch. He evidently thought the name sounded "fun, energetic and not scaring."

The name additionally likely profited by starting with an A, which implied it would be closer the front of any postings.

The Apple Logo

There are different hypotheses about the significance behind the name Apple. The possibility that it was named along these lines since Newton was motivated when an Apple dropped out of a tree hitting him on the head, is supported up by the way that the first Apple logo was a fairly confounded outline of Newton sitting under a tree.

Later the organization settled on the nibble out of an Apple structure for Apple's logo - a far less complex logo plan. These logos are most likely the purpose behind different speculations about the significance behind the name Apple, with some proposing that the Apple logo with a lump removed from it is a gesture at PC researcher and Enigma code-breaker, Alan Turing, who ended it all by eating a cyanide implanted apple.

In any case, as per Rob Janoff, the creator who made the logo, the Turing association is just "a superb urban legend."

Similarly the nibble removed from the Apple could speak to the narrative of Adam and Eve from the Old Testament. The thought being that the Apple speaks to information.

Selling the Apple I

Woz fabricated every PC by hand, and in spite of the fact that he'd needed to offer them for minimal more than the expense of their parts - at a cost at that would recover their cost as long as they delivered 50 units - Jobs had greater thoughts.

Employments inked an arrangement with the Byte Shop in Mountain View to supply it with 50 PCs at $500 each. This implied once the store had taken its cut, the Apple I sold for $666.66 - the legend is that Wozniak loved rehashing numbers and was unconscious of the 'quantity of the brute' conection.

Byte Shop was putting it all out there: the Apple I didn't exist in any extraordinary numbers, and the early Apple Computer Inc didn't have the assets to satisfy the request. Neither might it be able to get them. Atari, where Jobs worked, needed money for any parts it sold him, a bank turned him down for an advance, and in spite of the fact that he had an idea of $5,000 from a companion's dad, it wasn't sufficient.

At last, it was Byte Shop's buy request that did what needs to be done. Employments took it to Cramer Electronics and, as Walter Isaacson clarifies in Steve Jobs: The Exclusive Biography, he persuaded Cramer's chief to call Paul Terrell, proprietor of Byte Shop, to check the request.

"Terrell was at a meeting when he heard over an amplifier that he had a crisis call (Jobs had been tenacious). The Cramer chief revealed to him that two scruffy children had quite recently strolled in waving a request from the Byte Shop. Is it true that it was genuine? Terrell affirmed that it was, and the store consented to front Jobs the parts on thirty-day credit."

A unique Apple I (for a situation)

Employments was relying upon creating enough working PCs inside that opportunity to settle the bill out of the returns from pitching finished units to Byte Shop. The hazard included was unreasonably incredible for Ronald Wayne, and it's at last this that saw him duck out.

"Occupations and Woz didn't have two nickels to rub together," Wayne told NextShark in 2013. "On the off chance that this thing exploded, how was that... going to be reimbursed? Did they have the cash? No. Is it accurate to say that i was reachable? Truly."

Family and companions were reserved in to sit at a kitchen table and help weld the parts, and once they'd been tried Jobs drove them over to Byte Shop. When he unloaded them, Terrell, who had requested completed PCs, was astounded by what he found.

As Michael Moritz discloses in Return to the Little Kingdom, "Some vivacious intercession was required before the sheets could be made to do anything.

Terrell couldn't test the board without purchasing two transformers... Since the Apple I didn't have a console or a TV, no information could be channeled in or out of the PC. When a console had been snared to the machine despite everything it couldn't be modified without someone relentlessly composing in the code for BASIC since Wozniak and Jobs hadn't given the language on a tape or in a ROM chip... at long last the PC was exposed. It had no case."

A unique Apple I board, from the Sydney Powerhouse Museum gathering

Raspberry PI and the BBC's Micro Bit aside, we likely wouldn't acknowledge such a PC today, and even Terrell was hesitant at first at the same time, as Isaacson clarifies, "Employments gazed him down, and he consented to take conveyance and pay." The bet had satisfied, and the Apple I remained underway from April 1976 until

September 1977, with a complete keep running of around 200 units.

Their shortage has made them gatherers' things, and Bonhams sold a working Apple I in October 2014 for an eye-watering $905,000. In the event that your pockets aren't that profound, Briel Computers' Replica 1 Plus is an equipment clone of the Apple I, and boats at an unmistakably progressively moderate $199, completely manufactured.

When you think about that just 200 were fabricated, the Apple I was a triumph. It controlled its blossoming guardian organization to practically inconceivable rates of development - to such an extent that the choice to construct a successor can't have caused an excessive number of restless evenings in the Jobs and Wozniak family units.

The Apple II

Apple II

The achievement of the primary Apple PC implied that Apple had the capacity to proceed to structure its forerunner.

The Apple II appeared at the West Coast Computer Faire of April 1977, clashing with huge name rivals like the Commodore PET. It was a really momentous machine, much the same as the Apple PC before it, with shading designs and tape-based capacity (later moved up to 5.25in floppies). Memory hurried to 64K in the best end models and the picture it sent to the NTSC show extended to a really noteworthy 280 x 192, which was then viewed as high goals. Normally there was a result, and pushing it as far as possible implied you needed to satisfy yourself with only six hues, however dropping to an increasingly sensible 40 pushes by 48 sections would give you a chance to appreciate upwards of 16 tones at any given moment.

Indeed, the Apple II (or Macintosh][as it was styled) was a genuine development, and one that Jobs' biographer, Walter Isaacson, credits with propelling the PC business.

The inconvenience is, the specs alone weren't generally enough to legitimize the $1,300 cost of the Apple II. Business clients required motivation to plunge into their IT spending plans and it wasn't until certain months after the fact that the ideal reason introduced itself: the world's first 'executioner application'.

The first application on an Apple PC: Visicalc

Dan Bricklin

Dan Bricklin was an understudy at Harvard Business School when he pictured "a heads-up presentation, as in a military aircraft, where I could see the virtual picture [of a table of numbers] lingering palpably before me. I could simply move my mouse/console adding machine around on the table, punch in a couple of numbers, hover them to get an aggregate, do a few figurings... "

Obviously, we'd perceive that as a spreadsheet today, yet back in the late 1970s, such things existed just on paper. Changing over them for computerized use would be no little accomplishment, however Bricklin was unperturbed. He obtained an Apple II from his possible distributer and set to work, thumping out an alpha release through the span of an end of the week.

A considerable lot of the ideas he utilized are as yet commonplace today - specifically, letters over every segment and numbers by the lines to use as references when building formulae. (Thinking about how it looks at to Numbers today? Here's our Numbers audit.)

The innovative restrictions intrinsic in the equipment implied that it didn't exactly function as Bricklin had first envisioned. The Apple II didn't have a fused showcase and in spite of the fact that the mouse had been imagined it wasn't packaged with the machine. Thus, the showcase turned into the ordinary screen, and the mouse was swapped out for the Apple II's diversion paddle, which Bricklin portrayed as being "a dial you could swing to move amusement questions forward and backward... you could move the cursor left or right, and after that push the 'fire' catch, and after that turning the oar would move the cursor here and there."

It was a long way from flawless and working along these lines was lazy, so Bricklin returned to utilizing the left and right bolt keys, with the space bar instead of the fire catch for exchanging among flat and vertical development.

VisiCalc was disclosed in 1979 and depicted as "an enchantment sheet of paper that can perform counts and recalculations". We owe it an obligation of appreciation for the part it played in driving offers of the Apple II and securing Apple inside the business.

Writing in Morgan Stanley's Electronics Letter, in a matter of seconds before its dispatch, examiner Benjamin M Rosen elucidated his conviction that VisiCalc was "so amazing, helpful, all inclusive, easy to utilize and sensibly evaluated that it could well wind up one of the biggest selling PC programs ever... [it] could some time or another turn into the product tail that sways (and sells) the PC hound."

Source: https://www.macworld.co.uk/feature/apple/history-of-apple-steve-jobs-mac-3606104/

What made apple unique?

Apple wasn't the first nor the last company which was formed in the era to be able to reinvent the wheel when it came to computer technology. But many do not even know the names of the company which started during this same era and the reason is simply because they were neither unique nor could they last the test of time.

One of the reasons that apple stood the test of time much like us humans is that they kept evolving from the humble start that they got to the muti-billion dollar company they are today. In the whole history of Apple you will not find a single page that says that they were the same or stable as they were the last day. With their evolution they kept one thing stable in fact the only thing which is their promises to their customers- of a simplified and superior experience.

One of the reasons that Steve Jobs is still regarded as the best even today is the same reason. He ensured that as being one of the Management heads their promise to their customers lives the test of time and continues as the technology changed over the years or the way to use the technology.

Steve knew that it was this key factor which differentiated Apple from the rest and hence he has been seen quoting many times as,'Simple can be harder than complex: You have to work hard to get your thinking clean to make it simple. But it's worth it in the end because once you get there, you can move mountains.' and his other my personal favourite,'Be a yardstick of quality. Some people aren't used to an environment where excellence is expected.'

For him quality at work mattered the most yet he choose simplicity to represent it. From what I know about him, I know that for a presentation which he would give he would personally go through the list of all his attendees with their backgrounds, likes and dislikes to understand what to say and how to exclaim his points with references from the audiences life. He did it to be able to connect with them, reach them and get the reaction that he wanted from them.

How Zappos was Born:

Tony Hsieh is the CEO of Zappos.com, Inc. Amid the previous 10 years, the organization has developed from no deals to more than $1 billion in yearly gross stock deals, driven basically by rehash clients and informal. The following is an extract from Tony's expected book that depicts the start of Zappos.

Scratch [Zappos' unique founder] condensed his whole contribute three sentences: "Footwear is a $40 billion industry in the United States, of which index deals make up $2 billion. All things considered, web based business will keep on developing. What's more, almost certainly, individuals will keep on wearing shoes within a reasonable time-frame."

Half a month later, Nick reached us and said that he needed to set up a lunch meeting. He'd discovered somebody named Fred who worked in the men's shoe office at Nordstrom and was keen on joining the organization, however just if the organization got financing past the little loved ones round that Nick had effectively raised. Scratch likewise solicited me what I thought from "Zapos" as the name of for the organization, got from zapatos, which was the Spanish word for "shoes." I disclosed to him that he should add another p to it so individuals wouldn't misspeak it and unintentionally state ZAY-pos.

What's more, in this manner, the name Zappos was conceived.

A couple of days after the fact, Alfred [Zappos' present CFO and COO] and I met with Nick and Fred at Mel's, a 1950s-themed coffee shop a street or two far from where we lived. As we discussed the capability of Zappos, I did my best to not let the way that Fred was a spitting picture of Nicolas Cage occupy me from the business discussion. Fred was thirty-three years of age, tall, and truly looked like he could be Nicolas Cage's trick twofold.

I requested the turkey dissolve, with a side of chicken noodle soup to plunge the sandwich in. Fred requested a turkey burger. Precisely 10 years after the fact, Fred and I would come back to Mel's and request a similar thing to praise our ten-year meeting-versary together.

Scratch discussed the advancement that the site had made in the course of recent weeks. They were at that point getting $2,000 worth of requests seven days, and the numbers were developing. They weren't profiting, on the grounds that whenever a request was set, Nick would hurried to the nearby shoe store, purchase the thing, and after that transport it out to the client. Scratch needed to set up the site just to demonstrate that individuals would really purchase shoes on the web.

There were actually a large number of various brands in the footwear business. The genuine business thought was to in the end structure associations with many brands, and have every one of the brands give Zappos a stock feed of what was in every one of their stockrooms. Zappos would take orders from clients on the Internet, at that point transmit the request to the maker of each brand, which would then ship specifically to the Zappos client.

This was known as an "outsource" relationship, and in spite of the fact that it previously existed in numerous different enterprises, outsourcing had never been done in the footwear business. Scratch and Fred were wagering that they would most likely persuade the brands at the following shoe show to begin outsourcing, and after that Zappos would not need to claim any stock or stress over running a stockroom.

Fred revealed to us that he'd climbed the professional bureaucracy at Nordstrom for a long time, just purchased a house, and simply had his first child. He realized that joining Zappos would be a major hazard, yet he was prepared to go out on a limb an if Venture Frogs would give the seed financing to the organization.

Alfred and I took a gander at one another. Scratch and Fred were actually the sort of individuals we were hoping to put resources into. We didn't have the foggiest idea if the shoe thought would work or not, yet they were plainly enthusiastic and willing to put down huge wagers, so we were happy to wager on them as well.

Seven days after our seed speculation, Fred quit his place of employment at Nordstrom. He was authoritatively a Zappos representative at this point. He and Nick made a beeline for the shoe to appear in Las Vegas the following day.

"Conveying Happiness: A Path to Profits, Passion, and Purpose" is Tony Hsieh's first book, and has been released on June 7, 2010.

Source: https://hbr.org/2010/05/how-zappos-was-born-place-bets

What made Zappos unique?

Zappos was not the first and nor will be the last company who look at the footwear industry and say that they will start a new company to cater to it. The promise that zappos brought to the footwear industry was to convey happiness with a purpose.

Zappos is the first company who brought back the successfully ran with the outsource relationship wherein a customer on the internet would order a pair of shoes and Zappos would contact the brand makers and get the shoes on behalf of the client.

So outsourcing here was infact in the nature that Zappos would make the purchase for you on your behalf and send it over at your house.

How Amazon Got Started

The year was 94' and Bezos was working tirelessly on Wall Street. At 30 years of age, he started to see the web transformation happen, and settled on the choice to leave his place of employment and begin a web organization.

"The reminder was discovering this frightening measurement that web use in the spring of 1994 was developing at 2,300 percent a year. You know, things simply don't develop that quick. It's very uncommon, and that begun me about reasoning, "What sort of marketable strategy may bode well with regards to that development?"

In the wake of making a rundown of the 'main 20' items that he could possibly sell on the web, he settled on books in light of their minimal effort and all inclusive interest. It turns out, it was only the start... ..

The Founder's Start

As a kid, he spent summers at his granddad's farm in southern Texas, "laying channel, inoculating cows and fixing windmills". The 18-year-old Bezos "said he needed to fabricate space lodgings, carnivals and states for 2 million or 3 million individuals who might be in circle. 'The entire thought is to save the earth' he told the paper ... . The objective was to almost certainly clear people. The planet would turn into a recreation center".

Amazon's Funding

The underlying startup capital originated from his parent's close to home reserve funds.

From a meeting with Jeff Bezos, for the Academy of Achievement:

"The main introductory start-up capital for Amazon.com came basically from my folks, and they contributed a substantial portion of their life investment funds in what moved toward becoming Amazon.com. What's more, you know, that was an intense and confiding in thing for them to do on the grounds that they didn't have the foggiest idea. My father's first inquiry was, "What's the Internet?" Okay. So he wasn't making a wagered on this organization or this idea. He was making a wagered on his child, similar to my mom. Along these lines, I disclosed to them that I thought there was a 70 percent shot that they would lose their entire speculation, which was a couple of hundred thousand dollars, and they did it in any case."

Pursue on Funding

Amazon raised an arrangement An of $8M from Kleiner Perkins Caufield and Byers in 1995. In 1997, Amazon opened up to the world to raise extra capital. By 1999, the estimation of the Kleiner Perkins Caufield and Byers interest in Amazon made returns of over 55,000%.

A long time to gainfulness

Inside two months, Amazon's deals were up to $20,000/week. Notwithstanding, the organization has kept on furrowing their income over into development. The outline beneath delineates Amazon's proceeded with spotlight on long haul development, with benefit staying close $0 or underneath, and income rising.

Amazon Profitability

Imperative Amazon Milestones:

1994: Jeff Bezos leaves his place of employment and jump starts Amazon out of his carport.

Inside 30 Days, it is doing $20,000 every week in deals.

1995: Bezos raises a $8 Million round of financing from Kleiner Perkins.

1997: Amazon opens up to the world at $18 per share.

1999: Bezos is named Time Magazine's "Individual of the Year" for promoting internet shopping.

2009: Bezos gains Tony Tsieh's Zappos through a stock swap.

2013: Bezos gains the Washington Post.

Organizations Amazon Has Acquired:

Amazon has made more than 44 eminent organization acquisitions throughout the years. It's first Acquisition was in 1998.

1998: PlanetAll, Junglee, Bookpages.co.uk (later moved toward becoming Amazon UK).

1999: Internet Movie Database (IMDb), Alexa, Accept.com, and Exchange.com

2003: CDNow (Defunct)

2004: Joyo.com, an online business webpage in China.

2005: BookSurge, Mobipocket.com, and CreateSpace.com.

2006: Shopbop, a ladies' extravagance retailer.

2007: DPReview.com and Brilliance Audio.

2008: Audible.com, Fabric.com, Box Office Mojo, AbeBooks, Shelfari, and Reflexive Entertainment.

2009: Zappos, Lexcycle, SnapTell, Stanza (Kindle Rival).

2010: Touchco., Woot, Quidsi, BuyVIP, and Amie Street.

2010: Toby Press

2011: LoveFilm, The Book Depository, Pushbutton, and Yap

2012: Kiva Systems, Teachstreet, and Evi

2013: IVONA Software, GoodReads, and Liquavista

Jeff Bezos Startup Advice

"We are difficult on vision. We are adaptable on subtleties... . We don't abandon things effectively. Our outsider dealer business is a case of that. It took us three attempts to get the outsider merchant business to work. We didn't surrender."

"In case you're not difficult, you'll abandon explores too early. What's more, in case you're not adaptable, you'll pound your head against the divider and you won't see an alternate answer for an issue you're attempting to unravel."

Source:
https://www.fundable.com/learn/startup-stories/amazon

What makes amazon unique:
What made amazon unique is from their logo to the very point of what they deliver as a promise to their customer. They have always promised their customers smiles and hence they deliver that from the letter A to the last letter in the English alphabet Z they will cater to all the products and devices that their customer would want to deliver quality at your doorstep.

If it is not their uniqueness then what they thought would start as a humble online Bookstore today is the one-stop shop to almost all of their customer needs. Amazon hence is a true image of the thought that we need to be flexible and deliver value to our customers rather than our own pockets.

How Google Began?

The Google story begins in 1995 at Stanford University. Larry Page was considering Stanford for grad school and Sergey Brin, a student there, was assigned to show him around.

By some accounts, they disagreed about nearly everything during that first meeting, but by the following year they struck a partnership. Working from their dorm rooms, they built a search engine that used links to determine the importance of individual pages on the

World Wide Web. They called this search engine Backrub.

Soon after, Backrub was renamed Google (phew). The name was a play on the mathematical expression for the number 1 followed by 100 zeros and aptly reflected Larry and Sergey's mission 'to organise the world's information and make it universally accessible and useful.'

Over the next few years, Google caught the attention of not only the academic community, but Silicon Valley investors as well. In August 1998, Sun co-founder Andy Bechtolsheim wrote Larry and Sergey a check for $100,000, and Google Inc. was officially born. With this investment, the newly incorporated team made the upgrade from the dorms to their first office: a garage in suburban Menlo Park, California, owned by Susan Wojcicki (employee no.16 and now CEO of YouTube). Clunky desktop computers, a ping pong table and bright blue carpet set the scene for those early days and late nights. (The tradition of keeping things colourful continues to this day.)

Even in the beginning, things were unconventional: from Google's initial server (made of Lego) to the first 'Doodle'in 1998: a stick figure in the logo announcing to site visitors that the entire staff was playing hooky at the Burning Man Festival. 'Don't be evil' and 'The ten things we know to be true' captured the spirit of our intentionally unconventional methods. In the years that followed, the company expanded rapidly – hiring engineers, building a sales team and introducing the first company dog, Yoshka. Google outgrew the garage and eventually moved to its current headquarters (aka'The Googleplex') in Mountain View, California. The spirit of doing things differently made the move. So did Yoshka.

The relentless search for better answers continues to be at the core of everything we do. Today, with more than 60,000 employees in 50 different countries, Google makes hundreds of products used by billions of people across the globe, from YouTube and Android to Smartbox and, of course, Google Search. Although we've ditched the Lego servers and added just a few more company dogs, our passion for building technology for everyone has stayed with us – from the dorm room to the garage and to this very day.

These accounts are directly taken from, Source: https://about.google/our-story/?hl=en

The author of this book in no way claims any of the above content as his own.

How Google is unique?

Google was not started with an ideology of starting a company to make money and even today they stand by their that commitment. Google was started with a simple idea to simplify the online web and deliver value by bringing forth the highest value pages based on the users search history. If you can go back and see that though I am a third person in the context of all the above big companies but yet I have been able to write in their unique quality all in a line of two. I have been able to write their promises in two lines. This is the simplicity which matters and which makes even the most simplest of business to be able to grow bigger than their names and touch their millions of customers.

So while I do adjudicate big investment started industries it is the companies which can answer the question, Who? Are the ones who tend to go a long way as they are the ones which tend to quickly understand the changing demands of the users or Who and as per their change adapt to bring the same value to their customer and continue to grow.

How Starbucks began?

Thirty years ago, Howard Schultz got into the coffee business with one goal in mind: to enhance the personal relationship between people and their coffee.

He's now responsible for Starbucks, one of the world's most beloved brands, and worth at least $3 billion as chairman and

CEO of the Fortune 500 company. But it wasn't an easy path to the top.

How did Schultz, who came from a "working poor" family in the Brooklyn projects, overcome adversity and grow a quaint Seattle coffeehouse into the largest coffee chain on Earth?

Scroll through to learn the story behind Starbucks and its leading man.

Schultz was born on July 19, 1953, in Brooklyn, New York. In an interview with Bloomberg, he said growing up in the projects — "loosely described as the other side of the tracks" — exposed him to the world's wealth disparity.

He experienced poverty at an early age. When Schultz was 7 years old, his father broke his ankle while working as a truck driver picking up and delivering diapers. At the time, his father had no health insurance or worker's compensation, and the family was left with no income.

In high school, Schultz played football and earned an athletic scholarship to Northern Michigan University. By the time Schultz started college, he decided he wasn't going to play football after all. To pay for school, the communications major took out student loans and took up various jobs, including working as a bartender and even occasionally selling his blood.

After graduation in 1975, Schultz spent a year working at a ski lodge in Michigan waiting for inspiration. He finally landed a job in the sales training program at Xerox, where he got experience cold-calling and pitching word processors in New York. The work didn't fulfill him, so after three years he left to take a job at Hammarplast, a housewares business owned by a Swedish company called Perstorp.

There, Schultz ascended the ranks to vice president and general manager, leading a team of salespeople out of the US office in New York. It was at Hammarplast that he first encountered Starbucks. The coffee shop had a few stores in Seattle and caught his attention when it ordered an unusually large number of drip coffeemakers.

Intrigued, Schultz traveled to Seattle to meet the company's then owners, Gerald Baldwin and Gordon Bowker. He was struck by the partners' passion and their courage in selling a product that would appeal only to a small niche of gourmet coffee enthusiasts.

A year later, the then 29-year-old finally persuaded Baldwin to hire him as the director of retail operations and marketing. At the time, Starbucks only had three stores, but they were selling pounds of coffee for home use, Schultz said.

Schultz's career — and Starbucks' fate — changed forever when the company sent him to an international housewares show in Milan. While walking around the city, he encountered several espresso bars where owners knew their customers by name and served them drinks like cappuccinos and cafe lattes. Schultz had an "epiphany" the moment he understood the personal relationship that people could have to coffee.

In 1985, Schultz left Starbucks after his ideas to cultivate an Italian-like experience for coffee-lovers was rejected by the founders. He soon started his own coffee company: Il Giornale (Italian for "the daily").

In order to get Il Giornale off the ground, Schultz had to raise more than $1.6 million. "In the course of the year I spent trying to raise money, I spoke to 242 people, and 217 of them said no," he wrote. "Try to imagine how disheartening it can be to hear that many times why your idea is not worth investing in. ... It was a very humbling time."

Schultz spent two years away from Starbucks, wholly focused on opening Il Giornale stores that replicated the coffee culture he'd seen in Italy. In August 1987, Il Giornale bought Starbucks for $3.8 million, and Schultz became CEO of Starbucks Corporation. At the time, there were six stores.

America swiftly took a liking to Starbucks. In 1992, the company went public on the NASDAQ; its 165 stores pulled in $93 million in revenue that year. The world eventually caught on, and by 2000 Starbucks had grown into a global operation of more than 3,500 stores and $2.2 billion in annual revenue.

Howard Schultz StarbucksHoward Schultz, Chairman, Starbucks Coffe Company drinks the company's new product 'Starbucks Discoveries' during a preview party on September 26, 2005 in Tokyo, Japan. 'Starbucks Discoveries' is the company's first chilled cup coffee product which will be available at convenience stores on September 27 in Japan with the same coffee beans used at Starbucks stores.Junko Kimura/Getty Images

Thirty years ago, Howard Schultz got into the coffee business with one goal in mind: to enhance the personal relationship between people and their coffee.

He's now responsible for Starbucks, one of the world's most beloved brands, and worth at least $3 billion as chairman and CEO of the Fortune 500 company. But it wasn't an easy path to the top.

How did Schultz, who came from a "working poor" family in the Brooklyn projects, overcome adversity and grow a quaint Seattle coffeehouse into the largest coffee chain on Earth?

Schultz was born on July 19, 1953, in Brooklyn, New York. In an interview with Bloomberg, he said growing up in the projects — "loosely described as the other side of the tracks" — exposed him to the world's wealth disparity.

Schultz was born on July 19, 1953, in Brooklyn, New York. In an interview with Bloomberg, he said growing up in the projects — "loosely described as the other side of the tracks" — exposed him to the world's wealth disparity.

Source: Bloomberg

He experienced poverty at an early age. When Schultz was 7 years old, his father broke his ankle while working as a truck driver picking up and delivering diapers. At the time, his father had no health insurance or worker's compensation, and the family was left with no income.

He experienced poverty at an early age. When Schultz was 7 years old, his father broke his ankle while working as a truck driver picking up and delivering diapers. At the time, his father had no health insurance or worker's compensation, and the family was left with no income.

Source: "Pour Your Heart Into It"

In high school, Schultz played football and earned an athletic scholarship to Northern Michigan University. By the time Schultz started college, he decided he wasn't going to play football after all. To pay for school, the communications major took out student loans and took up various jobs, including working as a bartender and even occasionally selling his blood.

In high school, Schultz played football and earned an athletic scholarship to Northern Michigan University. By the time Schultz started college, he decided he wasn't going to play football after all. To pay for school, the communications major took out student loans and took up various jobs, including working as a bartender and even occasionally selling his blood.

After graduation in 1975, Schultz spent a year working at a ski lodge in Michigan waiting for inspiration. He finally landed a job in the sales training program at Xerox, where he got experience cold-calling and pitching word processors in New York. The work didn't fulfill him, so after three years he left to take a job at

Hammarplast, a housewares business owned by a Swedish company called Perstorp.

After graduation in 1975, Schultz spent a year working at a ski lodge in Michigan waiting for inspiration. He finally landed a job in the sales training program at Xerox, where he got experience cold-calling and pitching word processors in New York. The work didn't fulfill him, so after three years he left to take a job at Hammarplast, a housewares business owned by a Swedish company called Perstorp.

There, Schultz ascended the ranks to vice president and general manager, leading a team of salespeople out of the US office in New York. It was at Hammarplast that he first encountered Starbucks. The coffee shop had a few stores in Seattle and caught his attention when it ordered an unusually large number of drip coffeemakers.

There, Schultz ascended the ranks to vice president and general manager, leading a team of salespeople out of the US office in New York. It was at Hammarplast that he first encountered Starbucks. The coffee shop had a few stores in Seattle and caught his attention when it ordered an unusually large number of drip coffeemakers.

Source: "Pour Your Heart Into It"

Intrigued, Schultz traveled to Seattle to meet the company's then owners, Gerald Baldwin and Gordon Bowker. He was struck by the partners' passion and their courage in selling a product that would appeal only to a small niche of gourmet coffee enthusiasts.

Intrigued, Schultz traveled to Seattle to meet the company's then owners, Gerald Baldwin and Gordon Bowker. He was struck by the partners' passion and their courage in selling a product that would appeal only to a small niche of gourmet coffee enthusiasts.

Source: "Pour Your Heart Into It"

A year later, the then 29-year-old finally persuaded Baldwin to hire him as the director of retail operations and marketing. At the time, Starbucks only had three stores, but they were selling pounds of coffee for home use, Schultz said.

A year later, the then 29-year-old finally persuaded Baldwin to hire him as the director of retail operations and marketing. At the time, Starbucks only had three stores, but they were selling pounds of coffee for home use, Schultz said.

Source: Bloomberg, "Pour Your Heart Into It"

Schultz's career — and Starbucks' fate — changed forever when the company sent him to an international housewares show in Milan. While walking around the city, he encountered several espresso bars where owners knew their customers by name and served them drinks like cappuccinos and cafe lattes. Schultz had an "epiphany" the moment he understood the personal relationship that people could have to coffee.

Schultz's career — and Starbucks' fate — changed forever when the company sent him to an international housewares show in Milan. While walking around the city, he encountered several espresso bars where owners knew their customers by name and served them drinks like cappuccinos and cafe lattes. Schultz had an "epiphany" the moment he understood the personal relationship that people could have to coffee.

Source: "Pour Your Heart Into It"

In 1985, Schultz left Starbucks after his ideas to cultivate an Italian-like experience for coffee-lovers was rejected by the founders. He soon started his own coffee company: Il Giornale (Italian for "the daily").

In 1985, Schultz left Starbucks after his ideas to cultivate an Italian-like experience for coffee-lovers was rejected by the founders. He soon started his own coffee company: Il Giornale (Italian for "the daily").

Source: "Pour Your Heart Into It"

In order to get Il Giornale off the ground, Schultz had to raise more than $1.6 million. "In the course of the year I spent trying to raise money, I spoke to 242 people, and 217 of them said no," he wrote. "Try to imagine how disheartening it can be to hear that many times why your idea is not worth investing in. ... It was a very humbling time."

In order to get Il Giornale off the ground, Schultz had to raise more than $1.6 million. "In the course of the year I spent trying to raise money, I spoke to 242 people, and 217 of them said no," he wrote. "Try to imagine how disheartening it can be to hear that many times why your idea is not worth investing in. ... It was a very humbling time."

Source: "Pour Your Heart Into It"

Schultz spent two years away from Starbucks, wholly focused on opening Il Giornale stores that replicated the coffee culture he'd seen in Italy. In August 1987, Il Giornale bought Starbucks for $3.8

million, and Schultz became CEO of Starbucks Corporation. At the time, there were six stores.

Schultz spent two years away from Starbucks, wholly focused on opening Il Giornale stores that replicated the coffee culture he'd seen in Italy. In August 1987, Il Giornale bought Starbucks for $3.8 million, and Schultz became CEO of Starbucks Corporation. At the time, there were six stores.

Source: "Pour Your Heart Into It", Bloomberg

America swiftly took a liking to Starbucks. In 1992, the company went public on the NASDAQ; its 165 stores pulled in $93 million in revenue that year. The world eventually caught on, and by 2000 Starbucks had grown into a global operation of more than 3,500 stores and $2.2 billion in annual revenue.

America swiftly took a liking to Starbucks. In 1992, the company went public on the NASDAQ; its 165 stores pulled in $93 million in revenue that year. The world eventually caught on, and by 2000 Starbucks had grown into a global operation of more than 3,500 stores and $2.2 billion in annual revenue. Source: Starbucks

Starbucks' success made Schultz rich, and in 2001 he demonstrated his growing love for Seattle when he bought the Seattle Supersonics for $200 million. But the investment turned sour as the team struggled and Schultz feuded with players. In 2006, he sold the Sonics to a group of investors that moved the team to Oklahoma City, severely damaging his popularity in Seattle. He later called owning the team "a nightmare."

Running Starbucks came with set-backs, too. In 2008, Schultz temporarily closed 7,100 US stores in order to retrain baristas on how to make the perfect espresso. Over the next two years he led Starbucks' massive turnaround, with profits tripling from $315 million to $945 million by 2010.

As part of the overhaul, Schultz announced that Starbucks would aim to hire 10,000 military veterans and their spouses by 2018. Last year the company announced it would pay for employees' college tuition.

Throughout his career at Starbucks, Schultz has always prioritized his employees, who he calls "partners." Largely because of his father's experience when he was injured, Schultz offers all his employees (including part-time workers) complete health-care coverage as well as stock options.

In the last 28 years, Schultz has grown the coffeemaker to include more than 21,000 stores in 65 countries (ironically, there are none in Italy). "I've always been driven and hungry," Schultz said. "Long after others have stopped to rest and recover, I'm still running, chasing after something nobody else could ever see."

Schultz has parlayed Starbucks' extraordinary success into two books: "Pour Your Heart Into it: How Starbucks Built a Company One Cup at a Time"

(1999) and New York Times bestseller "Onward: How Starbucks Fought For Its Life Without Losing its Soul" (2012).

As Starbucks has continued to grow — it now has annual sales of more than $16 billion — so has Schultz's fortune. His net worth is estimated to be $3 billion. He revealed in "Pour Your Heart Out" that his tremendous professional success is a tribute to his late father, who "never attained fulfillment and dignity from work he found meaningful."

Source:
https://www.businessinsider.in/The-incredible-rags-to-riches-story-of-Starbucks-billionaire-Howard-Schultz/As-Starbucks-has-continued-to-grow-it-now-has-annual-sales-of-more-than-16-billion-so-has-Schultzs-fortune-His-net-worth-is-estimated-to-be-3-billion-He-revealed-in-Pour-Your-Heart-Out-that-his-tremendous-professional-success-is-a-tribute-to-his-late-father-who-never-attained-

fulfillment-and-dignity-from-work-he-found-meaningful-/slideshow/49487926.cms

This is the original text of the above article and again is in no way a work of the author writing this book.

How tesla began?

Tesla Motors probably shouldn't exist.

The last successful American car startup was founded 111 years ago. It's called Ford.

Barely a decade old, Tesla is already gigantic and adored. Its market capitalization hovers around $28 billion. Morgan Stanley calls it "the world's most important car company," and a 2014 nationwide survey found that Tesla's Model S was the "Most Loved Vehicle in America."

So how has Tesla flourished where others have flopped?

Today, everybody thinks Tesla was created by its charismatic CEO, Elon Musk, a PayPal cofounder who is the face of the company.

The truth is way crazier than that.

Tesla was the brainchild of a tiny band of obsessive Silicon Valley engineers who would go on to collaborate with - and collide with - the young billionaire.

This is the tale of that collision.

In reporting the story, Business Insider conducted several in-depth interviews with most of the key players and pored over little-noticed documents made public in a lawsuit. We also met with a curious lack of cooperation from the usually press-friendly Tesla Motors.

This is Tesla, the origin story.

Try And Touch The Dashboard
In the summer of 2004, a product designer named Malcolm Smith got a call from a hardware guy he used to work with, one Martin Eberhard.

"I can't tell you what we're doing," Eberhard said, "but why don't you come check out this car I have."

Smith headed over to Eberhard's tiny office in downtown Menlo Park, California. Eberhard and his partner, Marc Tarpenning, showed Smith a rough business plan and some rough specifications for a new car they wanted to build.

Not just any car: an electric car.

Smith was skeptical, quizzical, curious.

He realized that Eberhard and Tarpenning didn't need to reinvent physics; they just needed to combine barely available technologies to form a technological breakthrough.

"Well," Eberhard said, "let's go for a ride."

It felt handmade - because it was.
A decal on the side read "tzero," a reference to "To," a symbol that mathematicians use to denote the beginning of time within a system.

As they pulled onto Sand Hill Road, the now famous thoroughfare that's home to Sequoia Capital, Kleiner Perkins, and every other venture capital firm you've ever heard of, the hobby car was noticeably quiet.

Eberhard slowed the car to 10 mph.

"Try and touch the dashboard," he told Smith.

As Smith reached out, Eberhard hit the accelerator.

Smith's hand never made it to the dash. The tzero, an all-electric two-seater built by AC Propulsion, could leap from zero to 60 in under 4 seconds. G-forces threw Smith deep into his seat.

That's when it hit him. "I get it," Smith thought. "This isn't a nice little science experiment."

It was a highly technical vehicle.

No other car gives you 100% torque in an instant, he realized, but a high-performance electric ride does.

Another realization: Not all electric cars are clown cars or golf carts, even if the auto industry didn't have the will to show otherwise.

Smith would become one of the first 20 employees of Eberhard's new car company. His official title: vice president of vehicle engineering for Tesla Motors.

As Eberhard's young company grew, he'd continue to ask would-be recruits to touch the dashboard, before throwing them into their seats with the torque of an electric sports car, properly unleashed.

Source: https://www.businessinsider.in/The-Making-Of-Tesla-Invention-Betrayal-And-The-Birth-Of-The-Roadster/articleshow/45114983.cms

This is not the work of this author but just a humble re-presentation of what was written earlier in the (article link provided.)

18 Ways to Revive a Failed Product or Service

You likely recall a couple of well known item disappointments from similarly celebrated organizations. Google Glass, the New Coke, and the Ford Edsel ring a bell. However there are numerous renowned items that flopped yet later succeeded that don't really ring a bell.

Air pocket Wrap was made in 1957 as an in vogue backdrop. Truly. That item bombed so they attempted to showcase it as protection for nurseries and homes. That was better, yet it wasn't until IBM utilized Bubble Wrap to secure PC shipments that the item succeeded. At that point there's James Dyson, who starts creating and constructing 5,127 models of his acclaimed vacuum cleaner in 1979. In 1995, after dismissal by all the real makers, it at last turns into a top rated item in the UK.

These accounts of effective items that fizzled at first ought to effortlessly motivate us to take stock when looked with an item disappointment. Try not to devastate that extraordinary thought... at this time. It is in fact conceivable to re-dispatch a fizzled item or resuscitate a diminishing item. Also, if your business impulses are typically right, that is significantly more motivation to make sense of what turned out badly.

Break down Why Your Product or Service Failed or Why It's Dying

In one sense, no item is ever a total disappointment in the event that you get familiar with the exercises concerning why it fizzled. Information examination about the disappointment can tremendously enhance your client involvement with different items.

In How to Recover from a Failed Product Launch, Kissmetrics proposes the initial step is to break down the entirety of your measurements about the item dispatch itself. On the off chance that you use Google Analytics, that is a decent spot to begin. You can likewise get great knowledge from your contact the board framework and email stage. Gather information anyplace you can.

From that point onward, converse with and review your clients and target market to get input on the item. On the off chance that you use merchants, converse with them, as well. Once more, gather your item information anyplace and all over the place.

In the event that your examination persuades despite everything you have a feasible item, stage two is to redesign the item or potentially the showcasing. That is the place the diligent work starts. It takes a great deal of conceptualizing, mystery, and testing.

In view of that, here are 18 thoughts regarding how to renew a fizzled or blurring item.

1 - Give your item a name.

A name transforms an item into a brand and a brand has esteem. It suggests ability. It transforms the item into something that you, your customers, and your representatives can relate to.

Take a straightforward screwdriver set, for instance. What's all the more fascinating, a "Screwdriver Set" or "Pad Grip Screwdriver Set from Klein Tools?"

On the off chance that your organization is a perceived brand, or you possess a perceived brand name, use it. A "Specialist Screwdriver Set" from Sears has for quite a long time suggested polished methodology, quality, and lifetime execution.

Naming, a segment of marking, is a standout amongst the best approaches to resuscitate a fizzled item.

2 - Give it another name.

On the off chance that the item had a name the first run through around, attempt another one.

3 - Promote it utilizing media you didn't utilize the first run through around.

An excessive number of organizations limit their advertising message by adhering to what's typical in their industry, or by following what the other person is doing.

Obviously, your advertising should begin by characterizing your optimal customer(s) in incredible detail. At that point you discover where they can be achieved, where they hang out. Finally you utilize the media that will contact them.

I've seen organizations who, for example, just publicize on Facebook, or just in the paper, or just through a couple of other media. There is an immense range of media accessible through which you can pass on your item message. A short examining:

1. Magazines (print and computerized)
2. Online journals
3. Papers
4. Radio

5.   TV
6.   Neighborhood Events
7.   Web based life (Facebook, LinkedIn, Twitter, Instagram, Pinterest, and then some)
8.   Regular postal mail
9.   Public expos
10. Business Networking
11. Exchange Associations

Truly, it's a ton of work. You additionally should make sure you can follow every one of your endeavors in every medium, so you know your Return on Investment, or Return on Marketing Dollars. The result is justified, despite all the trouble.

4 - Change the item informing.

Maybe your item takes care of a genuine issue, a genuine client torment point, yet you're not passing on it. The client doesn't see it.

5 - Change the item deals technique.

change your item deals technique

On the off chance that your item is sold through direct salesmen, there could be an imperfection in your item deals procedure or a missing ability with the sales rep. A few signs that your business methodology may require refreshing or that you may need to broaden the business procedure:

• Your prospects still have the torment point your item can unravel. This returns to informing.

• Your prospect never said "No." Most individuals are extremely occupied at work and it's anything but difficult to get derailed. In the event that you surrendered following a half year, you may need to stretch out the business cycle to twelve.

• Your sales rep just had contact with one individual in the organization. Numerous organizations, even little ones, have more than one individual associated with buy endorsements. You may talk a supervisor or managerial individual, yet the proprietor composes the check once the person in question is persuaded of the need.

6 - Tell an anecdote about your item.

Take a gander at your client socio economics. Who are they? What age? What are their side interests and interests? Pay? Discover all that you can and compose another tale about your item that interests to that fragment. Or then again compose different stories to speak to every statistic section.

For example, when I sold items to the print completing industry, I enclosed the item by numerous "accounts" to speak to my prospects job in the association. A story from my very own history about such a large number of additional time evenings and ends of the week and demolished occasions spoke to the end-client on the processing plant floor. With our item they could stay away from the surprising extra minutes situation, still complete all their work, and appreciate a long weekend with their family. For chiefs I had stories and tributes about decreased client grievance and smoother creation with less exertion. For organization proprietors, I had stories (contextual analyses) enumerating their potential quantifiable profit, customer procurement, and customer maintenance.

Your client doesn't really relate to your item. Be that as it may, they DO relate to human battles that are like their own. That is the place your story comes in to play.

7 - Get another person to advance your item.

Discover a non-contender who benefits your objective market and check whether they'd be keen on adding it to their product offering.

8 - Find another item dissemination channel.

Regardless of whether you're moving direct or moving through a solitary circulation channel, consider including another wholesaler channel. Alternately, in the event that you just move through circulation channels, consider moving straightforwardly. Today, offering items direct is anything but difficult to do with the accessibility of online video, online courses, telephone calls, and robotized contact the executives frameworks.

9 - Offer your item to beta test clients at a rebate, or for nothing.

Utilize the input to enhance the item and get tributes.

10 - Do an item dispatch.

Dispatches make fervor and buzz that creates much a larger number of leads than an exhausting old item discharge.

On the off chance that you completed an item dispatch the first run through around, do your item dispatch investigation as we talked about above, re-vamp it and the item if necessary, and attempt another dispatch.

11 - Speak at occasions gone to by your optimal clients.

Public exhibitions, nearby business organizing gatherings, and instructing bunches all need speakers.

12 - Host an occasion that likewise includes your item.

You could create an instructive occasion that enables your objective to advertise take care of a particular issue. You could likewise co-have it with other non-aggressive vital accomplices.

For instance, on the off chance that you pitch a unique doohickey to auto fix shops, you could hold an occasion that instructs nearby auto fix shops how to fix more vehicles every day without procuring additional staff. Obviously, it would incorporate your thingamajig.

13 - Target an alternate market.

Examine your item's optimal client. Perhaps you focused on the wrong individual. The Bubble Wrap story is the ideal case of how to discover diverse markets for your items.

14 - Change your item valuing.

In the event that it's a vast item with a few segments or administrations, break it separated into discrete items. It's conceivable your optimal client doesn't require all that you offer, yet would cheerfully purchase the segments.

Alternately, attempt packaged evaluating in which you include other profitable, related items or administrations, for the most part offering a markdown for the group. Once in a while the expansion of administrations, for example, free technical support, maintenace contracts, or service agreements can help slacking item deals, particularly with unpredictable, specialized items.

15 - Get vital showcasing counsel from a business mentor or advertising consultant.

My proposal is to do this progression regardless. When we're excessively near the activity in our organizations, it's difficult to reevaluate and split away in new ways, regardless of whether a group is included. An outside counsel with a new point of view and no contending plans can rapidly observe things you and your group may miss.

16 - Examine the social foundation of your item target markets.

In Cashing in on Culture: Breathing New Life into Old Brands, the creator advises us that culture can represent the moment of truth an item. Dr. Inka Crosswaite expresses, "numerous South

Africans think lager in green jugs is 'posher' than brew in darker jugs, while the Greeks consider the classification the a different way."

We live in a multi-social world. We normally convey our social impacts and predispositions to those items and administrations we make. That is decisively why it's essential to inquire as to whether these impacts draw in or repulse our objective market, particularly on the off chance that we are moving globally.

17 - Get inventive, nearly to the point of insanity.

18 - Try an alternate visual search for your bundling and advancement.

Looks matter. On the off chance that conceivable, test a few plans. Not at all like years back, you don't need to spend much at all to get a lot of marvelous hand craft thoughts.

99designs is an intriguing method to get input from many creators, as appeared in the picture above, without employing them. You post a task ("challenge") and creators from around the globe present their fundamental plans for your item bundling. At the point when the challenge closes, you pick just the plan you like. The triumphant fashioner then completes the undertaking agreeable to you. In the impossible occasion that none of the plans bid to you, you don't need to pick a champ or pay for any of the entries.

I trust these 18 item recovery systems give you some significant takeaways.

Why the best brands believe in keeping it simple

So for what reason is being simple so vital? There are two reasons in my book:

1) It makes you center around being great at what you do.

2) It enables you to impart better to your valuable clients, staff and providers about what you're endeavoring to do.

Straightforwardness isn't anything but difficult to accomplish. Indeed, I for one think that its troublesome and have needed to buckle down at it. Refining thoughts into sound idea can require some serious energy and diligent work. I frequently state that it's lazier to compose a section than it is to keep in touch with one sentence.

Being succinct and making sense of how to improve is colossally fulfilling. Stripping back either a thought, look or usefulness to its center applies to all features of what we do. Be it web composition, item improvement, duplicate composition, how we converse with our clients or how we speak with one another in the workplace (maintaining a strategic distance from long gatherings is one genuine precedent!), keeping it straightforward is simply so essential that it merits propelling oneself that bit further to accomplish it. So here are my tips for keeping it basic:

1. Begin with a certain something and do it actually well.

There's an inclination to over-confuse in business, so oppose that allurement! Concentrate on being the best at that a certain something. Extraordinary organizations like Pret, Innocent or Apple have a solid comprehension of what they're great at and adhering to it. It's about business as usual, just on a bigger scale.

2. Work out the inquiry you're attempting to reply.

It might sound bizarre, however working out what the genuine issue or question is that you're endeavoring to illuminate, is in reality all the time harder than finding the appropriate response. This is especially the situation with imaginative things like promoting where you can get diverted distinctive energizing roads while overlooking the motivation behind the first message you are attempting to convey.

3. Try not to fear admitting to yourself that you're off-base.

When you have the appropriate response, test one methodology altogether - and if that doesn't work test another - to get to where you need to go. As opposed to having a go at everything on the double with the expectation that something – anything – will work. Be heartless with yourself and adhere to the point!

4. Tune in to your gut.

First considerations are typically right. In case you're over reasoning it, it likely isn't right. Hesitation or 'examination loss of motion's can be one of the greatest inhibitors for development. These are lost chances to test, learn and create as a business.

5. Wonder why?

For what reason should clients locate this fascinating? For what reason would it be advisable for us to do this? For what reason is this going to give us an arrival? I think when individuals get settled they can quit asking themselves this. And afterward they're in a bad position.

6. Does it breeze through the Mum test?

Since effortlessness is vital to making an incredible client experience, we use what we call the Mum test: is the site so straightforward that even my mum can utilize it? Would this pamphlet make her grin? Would she get what we're attempting to state? We've additionally joined our Head of Surfing's (otherwise known as website specialist) granny as one of our web analyzers! On the off chance that usefulness is instinctive for the non-well informed the probability is that most of clients will have a charming and simple experience as well.

7. Anticipate similar measures from others in your determined quest for effortlessness!

In the event that everybody is ready for a similar voyage it's increasingly viable, yet a mess of fun.

Business shouldn't be muddled and neither does the client experience: it's tied in with following certain tenets and utilizing decision making ability. Keeping it straightforward is a piece of each incredible business' DNA and furthermore a helpful system for your own rational soundness when running an organization! Diminish, decrease, lessen!

How simplicity can be achieved

Everyone is endeavoring to accomplish effortlessness, as is commonly said toning it down would be best however few of them know its genuine significance. A few people imagine that by evacuating overabundance stuff, they can make things basic. Content journalists feel that by lessening the extent of an article, straightforwardness can be accomplished.

Website specialists believe that by expelling undesirable beautification's they can accomplish straightforwardness. Be that as it may, decreasing the size or configuration isn't actually straightforward. Filling simply enough data, which is required, is known as effortlessness.

In the event that you are a fashioner, at that point diminishing structure components won't makes things straightforward, to accomplish effortlessness, one must put enough data, which is required at that situation. Beneath we will examine a few thoughts and tips, which can help you in accomplishing effortlessness.

Displaying a solitary thought

Numerous originators and specialists around the globe are always endeavoring to make a straightforward structure. To accomplish straightforwardness, one must focus on a solitary thought. Taking a shot at a solitary thought will help you focusing on the fundamental intentions. Along these lines, individuals can remain concentrated on a specific errand, and later they can move to the following stage, which can transform into something significant and lovely.

In the event that you plan a catch for sending messages and so on as GO or SUBMIT NOW, at that point them two are not appealing, and they are not notwithstanding portraying a reasonable message. Yet, in the event that you name that catch as 'Send Message', at that point it will turn out to be all the more certain that this catch is made for sending messages.

The thought behind this rationale is straightforward, you should work with paired methodology, which implies that you should leave clients with two decisions, yes or no. This parallel methodology is imperative, and it assumes a noteworthy job while making increasingly complex structures. Double methodology encourages you in accomplishing effortlessness, which is imperative in each structure. In this manner, a solitary thought essentially comprises of:

a. Paired methodology

This methodology leaves the client with two clear decisions, either yes or no.

b. Plain language

Language is vital while making anything. Plain and straightforward language encourages you in speaking with different clients. Plain language will help in making the structure basic and simple to utilize.

Improving clearness

In the wake of displaying a solitary thought, one must make sure to improve lucidity. Conveying a short and clear message is critical. For instance, in the event that you are building up an application, at that point making an alluring and engaging application isn't sufficient, you should stack a few highlights, which will profoundly intrigue the clients. You should not fill pointless data or highlights, which will befuddle the clients, and finally they will proceed onward without trying to check great highlights.

Data is required to make the point intriguing, yet on the off chance that you compose a lot about a similar subject, at that point perusers will in the end skip it and proceed onward to the following area. This is the place clearness is so vital. You should give data in all respects cautiously, expounding an excess of will obliterate the excellence, and cutting an excess of will likewise destroy everything.

Focuses referenced beneath will help you in improving lucidity:

a. Beginning and consummation focuses

Continuously ensure that beginning and consummation focuses ought to be alluring and engaging in the meantime.

b. Be engaged

Individuals at some point escape with the stream. These days, everyone wants to get drew in with short things. Continuously attempt to be engaged.

c. Clear bearings

In the event that you need to control somebody to subsequent stages, at that point direct cautiously with clear guidelines.

Be predictable

On the off chance that you are a designer, at that point consistency is extremely essential. A few applications are taken care of by new clients who need to utilize a straightforward application for quite a while. A few clients are long time clients, and they need overhauls, which can be aced effectively. Consistency will help you in making such application, which can be utilized by everybody. Consistency is essential, in the event that you need a straightforward plan since complex changes each time will leave the clients clear. Along these lines, in the event that you need something straightforward and appealing, at that point you should acquire consistency your plan.

When we are discussing consistency, we are really discussing the interface of any application. A few applications have a simple to utilize interface, and even subsequent to getting a few updates, the general interface continues as before.

Complex plans are additionally great, yet they should be kept for complex issues. Clients for the most part get confounded while utilizing complex things, and without an appropriate guidance manual they can't work it.

A few which helps in looking after consistency:

a. Comparable schedules

Keep in mind forget to utilize same procedure, which you utilized for before structures, this will help in keeping up the straightforwardness and consistency.

b. Example of creation

When you make something, which is motivated by past renditions, at that point recall forget to keep the interface comparable, this will help individuals while working any application.

c. Disrupting up the guidelines

In some cases, we should defy a few guidelines so we can concoct better structures. To accomplish straightforwardness, it's not essential to pursue each and every standard, you should disrupt a few guidelines to make something alluring and imaginative.

Accordingly, effortlessness can be accomplished by actualizing a solitary center thought with improved lucidity and consistency. In the event that these three standards are accomplished, at that point achieving straightforwardness is conceivable. Keep in mind forget that evacuating anything isn't straightforwardness. Including enough data at the perfect time is straightforwardness. On the off chance that you are an architect or an author, at that point effortlessness is the best thing, which you can offer to your customers. Effortlessness can be accomplished in all that we do in our everyday life.

My Key Takeaways from reading all about the successful start-ups

I believe that start-ups need to start from a humble start like an egg does. It has to be their force from the inside and steady growth that should be the driving factor in cracking of the egg and their opening to the world or announcing to the world that they are now open to do business at the global level.

During this whole process any start up must never loose focus on two things, the first their Who or their audience and why they thought to start up and if you intend to learn more on this than you can read my book, How the question, Who revolutionized marketing for me, available on lulu.com: http://www.lulu.com/shop/krishna-mohan-avancha/how-the-question-who-revolutionized-marketing-for-me/paperback/product-23981614.html

Your new start-up could be a copy of a successful one or just innovative and new to the market but what it should definitely be is just another means to annoy your customers or subscribers.

Yes, the life of an entrepreneur is not simple but it never was but the USP that you think your company or start-up should have needs to be simple and self explanatory in just two lines at max.

Warren buffet, is an American business magnate, investor, speaker and philanthropist who serves as the chairman and CEO of Berkshire Hathaway, says,'Never invest in a business you cannot understand.' and the people who make their biggest investments in your business is not you or your partners, Yes, you did invest time and money in your business but you did it to become independent and to live carefree. A customer invests their time, money and also ends up doing your marketing for you all for free if your product or service is of the highest quality. This is by far the largest investment more higher than any capital that a person could invest. It is this trust that helps small companies or start-ups grow to become a brand and lead their domain or service sector.

This is the same feeling that I hope to inspire in you reading this book through my writing. Aim for perfection but deliver a class or quality so par with your expectation that it leaves your Who or customer in awe as they were just expecting a product or service but not excellence which when delivered starts to define your brand.

All the companies noted in this book have achieved that and continue to do so. No really no one knows what a company or start ups true potential could be as a company with the most unique and working idea could just disappear due to multiple reasons while a company which is just a copy of the most working idea could become a brand and take the leadership position just due to the simplicity of their promise or working style.

Conclusion

Although the word brand in more the context of the consumer is limited to any company who is responsive, the word brand actually symbolizes any company that over time and regardless of the hour of day can be responsive with high standards of response. Brands will always go the extra mile for the customer. Marketing lost its way sometime back due to several factors including the need of business owner to start expecting marketing to bring in company revenue or profits.

I won't say that marketing cant be a profit making department of any company but the company needs to invest their time and money to enable it to do so.

There are two quotes that I firmly believe in,
"Our job is to connect to people, to interact with them in a way that leaves them better than we found them, more able to get where they'd like to go." – Seth Godin

"Make your marketing so useful people would pay you for it." – Jay Baer

So leaving you with these thoughts.
Hope to be able to share my thoughts.
Up until my next book.